United Nations Office for
Disarmament Affairs

UNODA OCCASIONAL PAPERS
NO. 16, APRIL 2009

ASSESSING THE UNITED NATIONS
REGISTER OF CONVENTIONAL ARMS

DÉPÔT
DEPOSIT

United Nations

As an exception to the normal *UNODA Occasional Papers* series, this publication is a specific contribution prepared by the Office for Disarmament Affairs to the 2009 Group of Governmental Experts on the United Nations Register of Conventional Arms. It may also be of benefit to those concerned with these matters in Government, civil society and the academic community.

Material appearing in *UNODA Occasional Papers* may be reprinted without permission, provided the credit line reads "Reprinted from *UNODA Occasional Papers*" and specifies the number of the *Occasional Paper* concerned. Notification to the following email address would be highly appreciated: unoda-web@un.org.

This publication is also available online at

www.un.org/disarmament

UNITED NATIONS PUBLICATION

Sales No. E.09.IX.4

ISBN 978-92-1-142269-6

Copyright © United Nations, 2009
All rights reserved
Printed in United Nations, New York

Contents

List of tables

Abstract

Confidence-building through reporting on conventional arms

If States behave in a predictable and transparent way, this may build confidence among them, and could help prevent conflict. One of the instruments to that end, which Governments can make use of, is the United Nations Register of Conventional Arms. It includes data provided by States on arms transfers as well as information on military holdings, procurement through national production and relevant policies.

Its aim is to foster regional and international confidence-building. Transparency in armaments can help to determine whether excessive or destabilizing accumulations of arms take place, may encourage restraint in the transfer or production of arms, and can contribute to preventive diplomacy. Since its inception in 1991, the United Nations Register has received reports from more than 170 States.

At its establishment, States decided that they would continue to work on expanding the Register's scope. They have done so through Groups of Governmental Experts. Such a Group is convened every three years and reports to the General Assembly, which may incorporate the Group's recommendations in a resolution. From February to July 2009, the United Nations Register is once again undergoing a triennial review by a Group of Governmental Experts.

This publication offers historical information on the Register as a tool of transparency, as well as points to possibilities for its future development. It also presents facts and figures related to the Register in convenient statistical graphs.

This paper was prepared by the
Conventional Arms Branch of the
United Nations Office for Disarmament Affairs

for further information contact: unoda-web@un.org

I. Introduction

THE UNITED NATIONS REGISTER OF CONVENTIONAL ARMS was founded when inter-State warfare had, for a long time, been considered the main threat to peace and security. It focuses on transfers of those major conventional weapons that typically can be used in offensive military operations carried out across international borders.

Present-day conflict has seen a progressive blurring of the boundaries between warfare, civil strife, rebellion, religious and ethnic clashes, commodities-related fighting and armed gang violence. Since the end of the twentieth century, front warfare and large-scale battle, which depend on major conventional weapons systems, have all but ceased to be the manifestations of conflict. In that light, the question naturally arises about the Register's added value in this changed global security environment.

The Register consists of seven categories and voluntary additional background information. All in all, States can report on the following:

I.   Battle tanks
II.   Armoured combat vehicles
III.   Large-calibre artillery systems
IV.   Combat aircraft
V.   Attack helicopters
VI.   Warships
VII.   Missiles and missile launchers
•   Information on military holdings
•   Information on procurement through national production
•   Information on relevant policies
•   Small arms and light weapons.

To expedite the reporting procedures, States are also encouraged to provide information on national points of contact (see box).

This paper sketches the continued relevance of the Register and the possibilities for further developing it. It may be seen as a basis for discussion in the United Nations Group of Governmental Experts on the Register, which is tasked to report to the General Assembly in 2009. As UN Member States will decide on the future of the Register, including a possible further expansion of its scope, this paper is meant to form a contribution to the debate.

National points of contact

The Register invites Member States to provide information on their national point of contact (NPC) and the expert groups periodically reviewing the Register have strongly encouraged them to do so. The standardized reporting form contains a section where this information can be provided. As indicated in that form, such information is only meant for governmental use.

Information on NPCs is important both for Member States and the Secretariat. It provides a channel of communication between suppliers and recipients enabling them to address possible discrepancies in reporting and to consult with one another on other issues.

Information on NPCs is also an important asset for the Secretariat, enabling direct contact to encourage the timely submission of reports, transmit documents and, when necessary, seek clarification of submitted information to facilitate the preparation of the Secretary-General's annual report and its subsequent document processing. In most cases, NPCs are based in capitals.

In recent years, the number of States that have provided such information has increased. The number currently stands at over 135, rising from 122 in 2006 and 82 in 2003.

II. Relevance of the Register

PATTERNS OF CONFLICT IN THE WORLD show a further erosion of the boundaries between different forms of violence, from military campaigns and insurgencies to sectarian violence and terrorist attacks. Also, a broader spectrum of actors may be involved: armies, private security contractors, armed rebels, terrorist groups and local-level power-brokers.[1]

This fragmentation of violence and diversification of armed actors has had some consequences for the types of arms used; e.g., small arms and light weapons have become the weapons of choice for much of contemporary conflict, and improvised explosive devices are increasingly applied by certain armed actors.

The predominance of mixed civil-military conflict and religious and ethnic clashes may lead to the assumption that the Register should focus on the types of weapons which are actually fired in conflict nowadays. However, that seems to be an incomplete approach. The Register covers international security in a broader sense. Member States reporting to it provide an insight into the build-up and volume of conventional arsenals which may help a State maintain a credible defence and perform effective peacekeeping tasks. By reporting, they are transparent about military potential; the Register does not deal with intention for use or actual use.

Therefore, the character of present-day conflict alone is not the only relevant factor for the Register — it is more about procurement needs in general. In other words, although armed groups may be prominently visible in armed conflict, States remain the dominant actors in weapons procurement and it is their overall conventional defence needs which the Register addresses. "Classical" national defence continues to be the driving force for the acquisition of military hardware; the conventional arms categories covered by the Register continue to be seen as relevant by contemporary armies. At the same time, the relevance of the Register would increase if it would take into account those conventional weapons that are most frequently used in contemporary conflict.

---

[1] See *SIPRI Yearbook 2008*, p. 43.

III. The Register's role as a confidence-building instrument

THE REGISTER WAS CREATED to discourage excessive and destabilizing accumulation of arms by making the quantity and type of arms transferred by States more transparent.[1] It was widely believed that transparency could contribute to confidence-building among States by reducing the risk of misperceptions and miscalculations about the intention of States that would likely arise in a non-transparent environment. If all States acquired arms in a transparent manner, they would be in a better position to determine whether excessive or destabilizing accumulation was taking place. Such an environment could also help to encourage restraint in the transfer and production of arms.

The Register's ability to achieve its declared aim will depend on its coverage of conventional arms, the data it is able to obtain and the extent of participation by States. Currently, the Register focuses primarily on transfers of seven categories of equipment that do not, for the most part, include combat-support systems, while global participation continues to fluctuate significantly, falling far short of the goal of universality.

Transparency of arms transfers is only one aspect of the concept of openness in military matters, as observed in the 1991 United Nations Study.[2] Confidence-building among States will also depend

---

[1] See General Resolution entitled "Transparency in armaments" of 9 December 1991, A/RES/46/36 L. This and all subsequent United Nations documents are available in the six official languages at http://ods.un.org.

[2] See the Secretary-General's Report entitled "Study on ways and means of promoting transparency in international transfers of conventional arms" of 9 September 1991, A/46/301, para. 97.

on the progress achieved in other areas, such as the United Nations reporting system for military expenditures.[3]

Primacy of major conventional arms in the Register

The General Assembly established the Register in 1991, as the outcome of an extended debate within the United Nations on the issues of conventional arms and transparency of arms transfers.[4] The seven categories it spelled out concentrated on major conventional arms. The consensus in the early 1990s was that the Register should focus on the transfer of conventional arms that could play a significant role in offensive military operations carried out across international borders. The Register's scope was also influenced by the Treaty on Conventional Armed Forces in Europe (CFE) between NATO and the former Warsaw Pact, which also focused on major conventional weapons.[5]

Brief history of transparency in armaments and the Register

League of Nations

International efforts to establish arms transparency as a global norm to help build confidence among States and promote restraint in the acquisition of arms stretch back to the early days of the League of Nations, the predecessor to the United Nations. Looking back at the competitive and uncontrolled trade in arms that fueled the outbreak of World War I, the League intended to negotiate a convention to regulate the global trade in arms and ammunition. In preparation, the Secretariat of the League was entrusted with the task of developing a standardized system for collecting and disseminating data on military matters in support of arms limitation efforts. Two Yearbooks were initiated. The *Statistical Yearbook on Trade in Arms and Ammunition*

---

[3] Established in 1981, the United Nations Standardized Instrument for Reporting Military Expenditures seeks data on defence spending by States on fiscal year basis. The Office for Disarmament Affairs manages this voluntary reporting instrument. For details, see http://disarmament2.un.org/cab/milex.html.

[4] Op. cit., fn. 1.

[5] With the exception of warships and missiles/missile launchers, the CFE Treaty contains all the other categories of the Register.

focused on international transfers of arms and ammunition of the League's members. The *Armaments Yearbook* covered the size, structure and inventories of their armed forces, their defence expenditures and economic potential for war. Launched in 1924, the Yearbooks of the League continued to be compiled until the outbreak of World War II.[6] The proposed convention, however, failed to materialize at the World Disarmament Conference in 1932.

The Register became operational in 1992 after its scope and procedures were elaborated by a Group of Technical Experts.

United Nations

After the founding of the United Nations in 1945, multilateral efforts to control conventional arms were initially focused on reductions in military holdings and limitation of the arms trade. In 1978, at the General Assembly's first Special Session on Disarmament, known as SSOD-I, States made a collective call for consultations to limit international transfers of conventional weapons.[7] But the focus on reductions and limitations generally proved to be too ambitious during the cold war period. The emphasis shifted to transparency as an instrument for building confidence and trust among States.

In 1988, the General Assembly agreed to devote more attention to the transparency of arms transfers.[8] As a result, a Secretary-General's expert panel was formed, which in its 1991 report advocated the establishment of a Register by the United Nations to promote transparency in conventional armaments.[9] The General Assembly embraced this recommendation.[10]

---

[6] The League of Nations Yearbooks are available at www.un.org/disarmament/ convarms/Register/HTML/Register_Resources.shtml.

[7] See "Resolutions and Decisions Adopted by the General Assembly during its 10th Special Session, 23 May-30 June 1978, A/S-10/4, paras. 81-85.

[8] See General Assembly Resolution entitled "International arms transfers" of 7 December 1988, A/RES/43/75 I.

[9] Op. cit., fn. 2.

[10] Op. cit., fn. 1. See also General Assembly Resolution entitled "International arms transfers" of 6 December 1991, A/RES/46/36 H, which reinforced the concept of arms transparency as a confidence-building measure and sought its promotion at the national, regional and international levels.

The Register became operational in 1992 after its scope and procedures were elaborated by a Group of Technical Experts.[11]

Military holdings, procurement through national production

Next to its seven central categories, the transparency of military holdings and procurement through national production were given a secondary status in the Register. Participating States in a position to do so could provide such information and if they did, it would be treated as "additional background information" pending further development of the Register. Reports submitted by States under these headings were not initially reproduced in the annual report of the Secretary-General but only indexed for reference and informal consultation by States interested in that information.

The change occurred at the 1997 review, when governmental experts agreed that reports submitted on procurement and holdings could be reproduced and, thus, made available to the public, unless the reporting State did not wish it to be reproduced.

Recurring review

When the General Assembly mandated the creation of the Register, it had also called for its subsequent review in order to assess the progress made and consider issues concerning its further development. The General Assembly specifically mentioned consideration of additional categories of equipment as well as modalities for bringing procurement through national production and military holdings within the fold of the Register.[12] For this purpose, it called for a review of the Register in 1994, after it had been in operation for two years.

To assist this process, the 1992 Panel of Technical Experts drew up a non-exhaustive list of equipment and proposed modalities for the Register's possible expansion, such as technical modifications to the parameters of the existing categories due to significant technological developments. It also proposed consideration of new weapons not yet

---

[11] See the report of the Secretary-General entitled "Report on the Register of Conventional Arms" of 14 August 1992, A/47/342.

[12] Op. cit., fn. 1, operative para. 8.

covered by the Register but worthy of consideration by virtue of their destabilizing potential.[13]

With regard to procurement, the 1992 Panel proposed that a number of questions be considered, such as, whether equipment assembled locally from imported components should be included or if produced through international collaboration by license.

Similarly, the Panel raised technical questions regarding what should constitute military holdings for the purposes of the Register and whether the reporting of holdings should be confined to the existing seven categories of equipment.

Since 1994, the Register has been reviewed at intervals of three years. While little progress was made in achieving consensus on its further development during the two reviews in the 1990s, the results have been more promising in recent reviews, when Governmental experts agreed to make the following modifications to the Register:

- The reporting threshold for large-calibre artillery systems was reduced from 100mm to 75mm, thereby bringing mortars within the purview of Category III of the Register.

- The threshold for reporting warships (including submarines) was reduced from 750 metric tons to 500 metric tons, thereby bringing other classes of naval vessels within Category VI of the Register, such as mine-sweepers.

- Category VII of the Register on missiles and missile-launchers was subdivided in order to include, on an exceptional basis, the reporting of man-portable air defence Systems, known as MANPADS.

The reviews also achieved some results of a procedural nature, such as:

- A simplified "nil" reporting form was adopted to encourage reporting by those States that did not have any transfer to declare, which helped to increase reporting by such States. An optional standardized form for reporting small arms and light weapons (SALW) transfers was adopted, which

---

[13] Op. cit., fn. 10, p.16.

has greatly facilitated the reporting of SALW transfers and helped to boost participation.

- The format was modified to obtain more information on the contact details of national points of contact.

These achievements have not exhausted the potential for the Register's further development. The agenda that has evolved through the review process contains other issues for further consideration, such as adding new categories, making further technical adjustments to existing categories, streamlining reporting procedures and deliberating on the status of procurement through national production, military holdings and SALW transfers, which currently fall under "additional background information".

Expansion of the Register's scope

When the 1991 United Nations Study recommended that the Register be established, it stipulated that it "should have the potential to expand to more comprehensive coverage, if required".[14]

The Register's possible expansion was also recommended by the 1992 Panel of Technical Experts, which offered a non-exhaustive list of military equipment that could be considered for inclusion in future reviews of the Register. The list, inter alia, included armoured vehicles designed for bridge-laying/launching, observation, reconnaissance, target indication/acquisition, electronic warfare or command of troops; air refuelling aircraft; and aircraft or helicopters designed for reconnaissance, electronic warfare and command of troops or for air-dropping troops.

One modality for expanding the scope of the Register was by making technical adjustments to the existing parameters of the seven categories with a view to enlarging the coverage of equipment under those generic categories. Another modality was to consider adding new categories. While additional categories could be considered, the Panel identified some key considerations:[15]

---

[14] Op. cit., fn. 2, para. 161.
[15] Op. cit., fn. 10, p.17.

- The focus should be on avoiding the "destabilizing" accumulation of arms;

- The impact should be of a significant nature on regional and international stability;

- Enhancing transparency should not prejudice the security of Member States;

- Enhancing the Register's scope should be based on substantial agreement to ensure the widest possible participation.

At the time of the Register's establishment, raising the status of reporting on military holdings and procurement through national production was considered an urgent issue that deserved specific attention in the deliberations of the Conference on Disarmament (CD) in Geneva. Similarly, issues such as transparency of nuclear weapons and the transfer of dual-use technology of military significance were referred to the CD.

Status of weapons of mass destruction (WMD)

Some States have been advocating from the outset that WMD, particularly nuclear weapons, should be incorporated in the Register and that dual-use technology of military significance should also be considered for inclusion. The main emphasis, however, has been on the transparency of nuclear weapons. At the time of the Register's establishment, the General Assembly had referred this and other related and unresolved matters to the CD.

Later, in 1999, the issue was revived when the General Assembly adopted a parallel resolution (54/54 I) that called for "the development of the Register in order to increase transparency related to weapons of mass destruction, in particular nuclear weapons, and to transfers of equipment and technology directly related to the development and manufacture of such weapons". The matter was discussed at the 2000 review of the Register, where an elaborate proposal was made for including nuclear weapons, related equipment, delivery systems, technology and facilities in the Register. However, the Group concluded that "the question of transparency in weapons of mass destruction was an issue that should be addressed by the General Assembly".[16] Nevertheless, the proposal was introduced again at the 2006 review. While recognizing the importance of transparency and its relevance to weapons of mass destruction, the Group reiterated the position adopted earlier in 2000.[17]

Small arms

It was the military build-up that fuelled the Persian Gulf conflicts in the 1980s and early 1990s that generated widespread concern about the destabilizing effects of transfers of major conventional weapons, as reflected in the 1991 UN Study. General Assembly resolution 46/36 L, under which the Register was established, contained several references to illicit arms trafficking but none to SALW. The seven categories it spelled out in its annex all dealt with major conventional arms.

In the late 1990s, as the issue of SALW gained prominence in the United Nations, the question of possibly including them in the Register was examined, especially after the adoption of the 2001 UN Programme of Action on the illicit trade in SALW, which did not cover the transparency of licit SALW transfers. As a result, the optional reporting of SALW transfers was first introduced in 2003 when the Expert Group reviewing the Register agreed that SALW transfers could be reported by interested States, that were in a position to do so, as part of additional background information, as was the case with procurement and holdings.

In a significant development, the Expert Group reviewing the Register in 2006 agreed on a standardized format that could be used for reporting SALW transfers on an optional basis but, as before, under the rubric of "additional background information". The language of the 2006 report was also more positive on SALW than was

---

[16.] See the note by the Secretary-General entitled "Continuing operation of the United Nations Register of Conventional Arms and its further development" of 9 August 2000, A/55/281, para. 90.

[17] See the note by the Secretary-General entitled "Continuing operation of the United Nations Register of Conventional Arms and its further development" of 15 August 2006, A/61/261, para. 107.

the more tentative language of the 2003 report.[18] For example, the 2006 Group noted that "there was no transparency instrument covering international transfers of SALW between States, although those transfers were believed to comprise a significant portion of the global trade in conventional weapons".[19]

---

[18] See the note by the Secretary-General entitled "Continuing operation of the United Nations Register of Conventional Arms and its further development" of 13 August 2003, A/58/274.

[19] Ibid., para.103.

IV. Participation in the Register

Global level

THE REGISTER MADE A PROMISING START when it went into operation in 1992 by receiving reports from 95 States, including all of the permanent members of the Security Council and most major producers, exporters and importers of conventional arms. This was more than what some observers had expected, given the traditional sensitivity of many States to disclosing information on military matters on grounds of national security. (See Table 1).

The level of participation fluctuated to some extent during the 1990s, averaging at 94, including some retroactive submissions later solicited by the Secretariat. During this period, the highest level recorded was 100 for calendar year 1999, while the lowest level was 85 for 1998. During the next decade, the participation increased significantly from 118 for 2000 to the highest point, so far, of 126 for 2001. Nevertheless, the average level of participation since the year 2000 remains at 115 because the number of submissions for the latest calendar year, 2007, has fallen short of the previous years (91 reports).

Even though the participation level has fluctuated, sometimes significantly, and universality remains a distant goal, 170 Member States have reported to the Register at least once since its inception. Perhaps more importantly, the Register now enjoys regular participation by all permanent members of the Security Council and almost all the major producers, exporters and importers of conventional weapons report on a consistent basis. Indeed, the Register also captures arms transfers involving many States that do not submit reports, as they are reflected in the submissions by the reporting States in their capacity as exporters or importers. Thus, for example, while 123 States reported for 2002, the Register was able to capture transfers involving 27 non-reporting countries, including some that had never participated in the

Register. The Register may, therefore, reflect a large bulk of transfers of conventional arms under its seven categories of equipment. Nevertheless, the pattern of participation has varied significantly, showing a lack of consistency. Therefore, a wide gap has remained between the global average and the goal of universality.

Table 1: Global participation

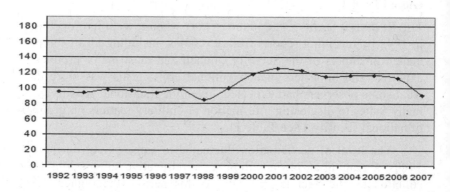

Regional level

In recent years, participation has been relatively stable in some regions while not in others, thereby contributing to the variations in the global total. (The regional groupings are the same as those established for General Assembly elections).

Participation by States from *Africa* averaged at 9 during the 1990s, from a high of 13 for 1992 and to its lowest level so far, of 3 for 1998. The average level since 2000 has been 14, from a low of 8 for 2007 to its highest point yet, of 17 for 2001 and 2002. With a total of 53 Member States from Africa, participation from that region during the 1990s averaged at 17 percent, while the average since 2000 has been 26 percent. The lowest and highest levels so far have been under 6 percent and 32 percent, respectively (see Table 2).

Participation by States from *Asia* averaged at 24 during the 1990s, from a high of 27 for 1995 to its lowest level thus far, of 21 for 1998. The average level since 2000 has been 29, from a low of 21 for 2007 to the highest point, so far, of 32 for 2003. With a total of 53 Member States from Asia, participation from that region during the 1990s averaged at about 45 percent, while the average since 2000 has been close to 55 percent. The lowest and highest levels so far have been approximately 40 and 60 percents, respectively (see Table 3).

Participation by States from *Latin America and the Caribbean* averaged at 16 during the 1990s, from a high of 21 for 1999 to a low of 13 for 1998. The average level since 2000 has been 20, from its lowest point thus far, of 11 for 2007 to its highest level, so far, of 26 for 2001. With a total of 33 Member States from Latin America and the Caribbean, participation from that region during the 1990s averaged at 48 percent, while the average since 2000 has been over 62 percent. The lowest and highest levels thus far have been over 33 percent and close to 79 percent, respectively (see Table 4).

Participation by States from *Eastern Europe* averaged at 16 during the 1990s, from a high of 18 for 1996 and 1998 to its lowest so far, of 14 for 1993. The average level since 2000 has been 21, from a low of 20 for 2003 to its highest point yet, of 22 for 2002, 2006 and 2007. With a total of 23 Member States from Eastern Europe, participation from that region during the 1990s averaged at about 73 percent, while the average since 2000 has been approximately 95 percent. The lowest and highest levels thus far have been about 64 and 100 percents, respectively (see Table 5).

Participation by States from *Western Europe and Others* averaged at 28 during the 1990s, from a high of 30 for 1997, 1998 and 1999 to its lowest point so far, of 26 for 1993. The average level since 2000 has been close to 30, from a low of 29 for 2002, 2004 and 2007 to a high of 30 for 2000, 2001, 2003, 2005 and 2006. With a total of 30 Member States from Western Europe and Others, participation from that region during the 1990s averaged at 93 percent, while the average since 2000 has been over 98 percent. The lowest and highest levels thus far have been about 86 and 100 percents, respectively (see Table 6).

Regional participation

Table 2: *Africa*

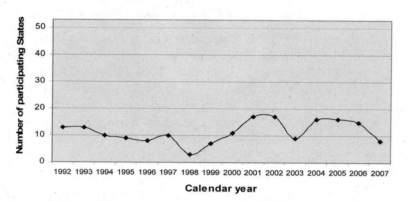

Table 3: *Asia*

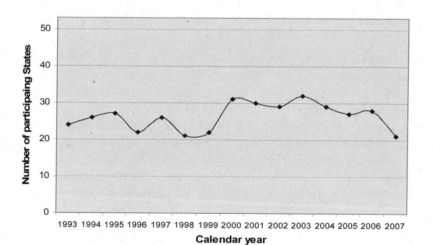

Table 4: *Latin America and the Caribbean*

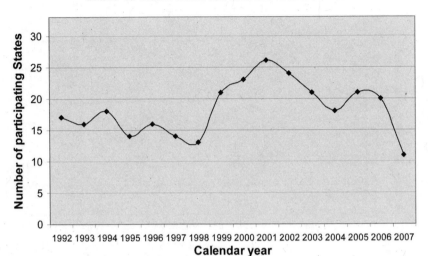

Table 5: *Eastern Europe*

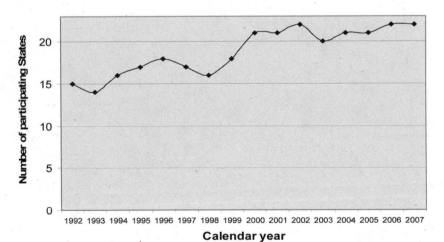

Table :6 *Western Europe and other States*

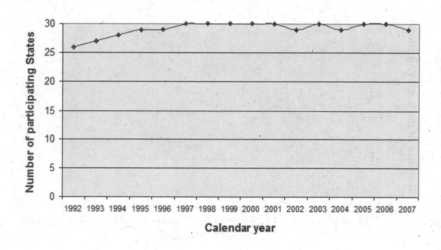

V. Transparency achieved by the Register

THE UNITED NATIONS REGISTER OF CONVENTIONAL ARMS STANDS OUT AS A UNIQUE SOURCE OF DATA on the quantity and type of conventional arms exported or imported. Other sources are based primarily on the monetary value of annual transfers, which are usually aggregated to cover all categories of arms. Furthermore, their estimates are ballpark figures and are sometimes significantly at variance with each other, thus making monetary estimates a less reliable indicator of the magnitude of arms accumulation than assessments based on quantity and type.

However, for more comprehensive data on quantity and type in its seven categories of equipment, the Register needs to bridge significant gaps. Arms transfers are the primary focus of the Register and the degree of transparency achieved in this area depends on the extent to which the States provide full information according to the standardized reporting system.

The reporting format for submitting returns on arms transfers contains an optional "Remarks" column, which reporting States are encouraged to use to provide details of the transfer declared under the seven generic categories listed in the reporting form. The "Remarks" column contains two sub-columns, one entitled "Description of item" and other "Comments on transfer". The sub-column on "Description of item" is particularly important as it seeks detail on the type and model of equipment transferred. Almost all reporting States have been using the "Remarks" column in their submissions except in some cases, which are mostly related to missiles and missile-launchers. Since the Register's inception, there has been some sensitivity to the full disclosure of information under this category on grounds of security sensitivity. The absence of full disclosure could mean that either the quantity has not been disclosed or the type and model are not specified.

Since this deficiency is limited to a few States, it could be said that, for the most part, the Register fulfils the objective of transparency under the existing system of reporting on arms transfers. Nevertheless, the data contained in the Register cannot be considered comprehensive. Additionally, transfers involving non-participating States that are exporters and importers in the same transaction would not be captured. Thus, the Register cannot reliably capture all the transfers covering its seven categories nor necessarily provide full data on the type and quantity of transfers reported to it.

Similarly, with regard to the second tier of transparency related to procurement, military holdings and SALW transfers, thus far, the Register has achieved a limited degree of progress. While some States that produce major weapons systems do not report their national procurement to the Register, an even greater number of States do not report their military holdings. The pattern of reporting on procurement shows that an average of 22 States disclosed their domestic acquisition since 1992; the highest number of 29 was recorded for 2000 and 2001, while the lowest number was 11 for 1992. For 2007, the number of reporting States was 19 (see Table 7). With regard to holdings, most States maintain regular armed forces and their inventories include one or more of the seven categories of equipment covered by the Register. However, to date, the average level of reporting on holdings has been 30 since 1992, with the highest point of 35 for 2000 and the lowest point of 23 for 1992. For 2007, the number of States disclosing their military holdings was 26.

Reporting of SALW transfers has increased substantially, rising from 5 States for 2003, after SALW transfers were included in the Register, to 37 and 48 States in 2007 and 2008 respectively, after the standardized reporting form was adopted in 2006. The reporting of small arms and light weapons (SALW) transfers for the latest calendar year 2007 has increased further both in terms of the number of reporting States, the details of their transfers and the diversity of countries submitting reports. The progress achieved on SALW transfers over the past two years has imparted an additional dimension to the Register's value as a source of data on arms transfers. Continued progress in this area will further strengthen its value (see Table 8).

Table 7: Procurement through national productin and military holdings

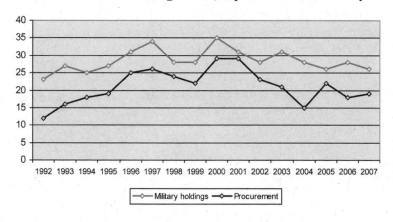

Table 8: International transfers of SALW

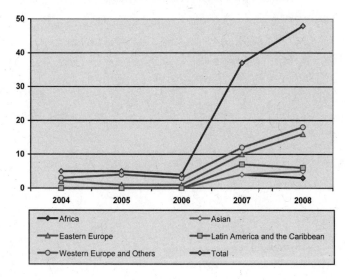

VI. Points of contention in the past

WHILE GOVERNMENTAL EXPERTS REVIEWING THE REGISTER were able to agree and make progress on some issues, there are other issues, both generic and specific, on which they have deliberated at length but without reaching a conclusion or resolution.

The technical adjustments made to some categories of equipment have enlarged the Register's scope to some extent. Small arms and light weapons (SALW) transfers have also been brought within the Register's framework, and an optional standardized reporting form enables interested States to utilize a common method of reporting. Procedural refinements have been made to encourage "nil" reporting by States and more emphasis has been placed on the importance of information on national points of contact.

On the other hand, consensus has not yet proved possible on all issues, including the following:

- A standardized form for reporting procurement through national production, including a provision for "nil" reporting;

- Lowering further the reporting threshold for warships and submarines;

- Technical adjustments to incorporate combat-support functions in some of the existing categories (armoured combat vehicles, combat aircraft and attack helicopters);

- Clarifying the status of unmanned aerial vehicles (UAVs) that perform combat roles;

- The possible inclusion of surface-to-air missiles, known as SAMs;

- Creating an eighth category to incorporate SALW within the main scope of the Register;

- Bringing "additional background information" on par with international transfers of major conventional weapons; and

- Agreed management of clarification requests and mismatches.

With regard to reporting on procurement, a number of States producing major conventional arms make submissions to the Register regularly, while some others are reluctant to do so either because they consider it too sensitive from their national security perspective or because they are reluctant to disclose such data unless all the major producers do so, as well as other States that are of particular interest to them.

The sensitivity with regard to reporting on military holdings has been distinctly greater, which partly accounts for the limited attention its status has received in the previous reviews.

The Register's role in arms embargoes

The Register was not designed to support arms embargoes sanctioned by the Security Council. Some limiting factors would include:

- The Register is a voluntary reporting system. If it would become a tool for monitoring an arms embargo, all exporting and importing nations would have to report their transfers to determine whether any prohibited equipment has been transferred.

- Since the Register covers seven categories of combat-systems, its value would be restricted if the scope of the arms embargo were to exceed those categories.[1]

- Transfers of transport aircraft, helicopters, UAVs, utility vehicles (which could be subsequently modified for combat, as has happened frequently) and other conventional weapons systems are not covered by the Register's categories.

---

[1] Most arms embargoes, mandatory or non-mandatory, sanctioned by the Security Council have referred to all types of arms and ammunition, thus greatly exceeding the major weapons covered by the Register. The arms embargo imposed on the Democratic People's Republic of Korea in 2006, however, focused on the seven categories of the Register, S/RES/1718 (2006).

- Imported kits from which a weapons system can be assembled do not have to be reported.

- The reporting of SALW transfers is optional.

- Another limiting factor could be the time it takes for the transfer to be reported to the Register — there could be a significant time lag. Thus, a transfer that hypothetically took place in February 2009, could be reported to the Register by as late as October 2010.

However, in the context of Security Council arms embargoes, the value of the Register is being increasingly noticed — if not yet for monitoring a current embargo, then as a tool for assessing the military hardware needs of a State coming out of conflict and closing in on the end of its embargo. Both Groups of Experts on Côte d'Ivoire and Sudan have separately recommended that each State submit a baseline assessment of their arms acquisitions and holdings to the Register.[2]

---

[2] See the report of the Secretary-General entitled "Small Arms" of 17 April 2008, S/2008/258.

VII. Further development of the Register

Military holdings and procurement through national production

As yet, the Register has no standardized system for the optional reporting of procurement and holdings. The regular General Assembly resolution on the Register only requests that such reports include information on type and model of equipment by using the "Remarks" column when States report on international transfers.[1]

The reporting of military holdings has received limited attention during reviews of the Register, in part because many States continue to be sensitive about disclosing their holdings. The issue of developing a standardized form for reporting procurement and bringing it on par with international transfers has received more attention recently, most notably in the 2006 review.

Small arms

The United Nations study of 1991 that recommended the establishment of the Register did not contain a specific reference to small arms and light weapons (SALW), except for a fleeting reference made in the context of drug traffickers, terrorist groups and other clandestine organizations. Otherwise, it only contained references to "illicit arms trafficking", which could be regarded as implicitly encompassing SALW.

While major conventional weapons remain a continuing concern as they affect threat perceptions among States, and significant resources are incurred in their development and acquisition, inter-State

---

[1] For an example, see "Transparency in armaments" of 18 December 2006, operative para. 5, A/RES/61/77. This and all subsequent General Assembly resolutions are available at http://ods.un.org.

armed conflicts have declined since the 1990s.[2] The proliferation of armed non-State groups around the world, the use of non-traditional methods of warfare and the nexus between such groups and globally organized crime syndicates, especially drug-trafficking networks, suggest that light weapons will continue to impact significantly on national, regional and international security. There is nothing in the criteria for the further development of the Register set out in these documents that precluded the inclusion of SALW.

Progress towards universal participation

One reason for the unsteady progress in participation has been that some States have been less consistent in reporting each year than others. This is evident from the fact that while the average level of participation each year has less than 120 States, the number that have reported to the Register at least once stands at 170 (even though some later withdrew their participation over the issue of weapons of mass destruction). There could be various reasons for inconsistent reporting, which are not easy to identify with certitude, but in a number of cases the factors behind inconsistency are more likely to be bureaucratic than political. For example, changes in the bureaucracy resulting in the loss of personnel familiar with the Register can also sometimes cause disruption in the system associated with the submission of reports.

While inconsistency is a major factor, it is not the only reason for the Register's limited progress towards universal participation. In some cases, States have not reported to the Register for lack of techni-cal or institutional capacity or for reasons of political sensitivity at a time of conflict or crisis. States in conflict, even if they have the capacity to file reports, may be reluctant to do so if they believe that disclosing their acquisition might put their adversaries at an advan-tage. In most cases, States in conflict situations have not reported to the Register.

A more enduring reason for non-participation by a number of States, which dates back to the early 1990s, has been their conten-

---

[2] For an example of the changing pattern of armed conflicts, see the conflict database of the Centre for International Development and Conflict Management, Uppsala University, Sweden, at http://www.pcr.uu.se/database.

tion that the Register should be a more comprehensive instrument of transparency, covering not only conventional arms but also weapons of mass destruction and dual-use technology of military significance.

Participation

The progress of the Register in terms of participation remains an important issue. As indicated earlier, while the average number of States reporting to the Register has increased significantly over the past seven years, as compared to the preceding eight years, it is far from universal. There has also been fluctuation in participation over time, which has introduced an element of unpredictability or uncertainty. Realistically, universal participation should perhaps be seen as a long-term goal, as the Register is a voluntary reporting instrument. There are issues impeding the participation of some States that may either fall outside the purview of the Register or may not be amenable to consensus in the near future. Nevertheless, the average level of participation would rise significantly if States would be persuaded to report on a more consistent basis. In most cases, these may be States that are potential "nil" reporters. (See Table 9 below).

Table 9: Reports on transfers and "nil" returns

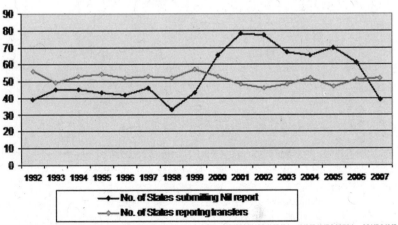

connicts that have suffered a loss of institutional capability, which may account for their lack of participation. Capacity-building in such cases may involve technical training of key personnel as part of institutional rebuilding of the security sector.

Many reports are submitted well after the nominal deadline of 31 May and, therefore, cannot be reflected in the annual consolidated report of the Secretary-General, except in subsequent addenda to that report (see Table 10 below). This may require a review of internal arrangements by States to see how submissions could be expedited.

Table 10: Reporting by 31 May deadline

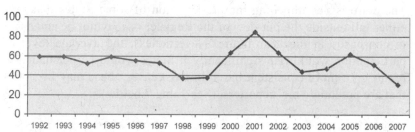

Other substantive and procedural issues

Further development of the Register in terms of its scope is an ongoing process that was initiated at the outset. Apart from the substantive question of bringing procurement and holdings on par with international transfers, there is a pending procedural issue of providing a standardized system for reporting under these headings, even on an optional basis. A standardized reporting system should present fewer difficulties since it would not prejudge the substantive issue of bringing "additional background information" on par with international transfers. Furthermore, a standardized reporting system for procurement and holdings would be unavoidable if Member States wish to file their annual returns directly to the Register.[3] Technically,

---

[3] The Office for Disarmament Affairs is currently implementing a pilot project to test the feasibility of direct electronic filing of reports by Member States to the Register.

a standardized format would also help to make the Register's public database more user-friendly.

Likewise, the Register could strengthen its value as a source of hard data on quantity and type of equipment transferred if some gaps can be bridged, particularly with regard to the transfer of missiles and missile-launchers. One approach might be to consider integrating the "Remarks" column into the core reporting form by removing the space that physically separates it. However, this would require changing the structure of the reporting system as well as reversing an understanding on the reporting of missile transfers, even though, in practice, only a few States have been reluctant to disclose quantity or type.

Another possible refinement may be to accompany export and import information with data on arms to be taken from service (in the seven agreed categories).

A further option to improve the practical use of the Register may be to consider that information on export and import of conventional arms, including SALW, be accompanied in the "Remarks" column by data on the relevant end user certificate(s).

Member States could also consider some purely procedural changes to make the reporting of transfers clearer than it is currently. The format for reporting missiles and missile-launchers includes a subcategory "(b)" for man-portable air defense systems, known as MANPADS. In some submissions, it is difficult to distinguish between entries for the two subcategories, thereby reducing the transparency value of transfers reported under this category. A clearer distinction between the two subcategories in the standardized reporting forms would be desirable; a proposal thereto could be suggested by the United Nations Secretariat.

Similarly, sometimes it is not easy for the observer to align the number of transfers declared under a particular category with the information provided on the type and model of those reported numbers. Perhaps, a further refinement of the format to visually separate the entries within each category could be considered.

As abbreviations can sometimes be confusing or difficult to interpret with certainty, defining those used in national reports, in an attachment, would expedite the preparation of the Secretary-General's annual report. It would also help to avoid distortions when they are translated from the original language into the other official UN languages.

Discrepancies or mismatches between exports and imports continue to occur in the reports on transfers, as earlier observed by the 2006 Group of Governmental Experts. This makes it difficult to determine with certainty the quantities of equipment transferred in a given year.

Consultations between suppliers and recipients, in all instances prior to the reporting of transfers, would help to reduce mismatches. However, as discussed in the previous reviews, mismatches occur mainly because of differences in the definition of "transfer". As such, to eliminate discrepancies as far as possible, perhaps a renewed effort should be considered to examine the prospects of a common definition, thus enhancing the Register's reliability as a source of data. Also, a light arrangement for formal clarification requests can be considered, for instance, through the United Nations Secretariat.

Since the Register's inception, extra-budgetary resources to support regional workshops have been an essential part of its pro-motional effort. A series of seminars held in the early 1990s played a major role in giving the Register a promising start. Likewise, a number of workshops held during 2001-2006 helped not only to promote the Register but also to obtain valuable feedback for the 2003 and 2006 reviews. The Register would benefit greatly from the continued avail-ability of extra-budgetary funds to organize workshops, as there are no provisions in the regular budget for that exercise.

As the pattern of regional reporting shows, there is a need to sustain the workshop series in some regions more than in others to encourage a higher, or at least a more consistent, level of participation at the regional or subregional levels, and also to raise the profile of the Register at those levels.

The workshop mechanism is also essential for another reason. Since the Register is reviewed periodically, regional workshops provide an important channel of communication to obtain feedback for subsequent reviews. This is particularly important since Groups of Governmental Experts are quite limited in size, which means that most States are not able to have a direct impact on the review process.

In practice, fund-raising to generate extra-budgetary resources has been an arduous undertaking, at least partly because there are many competing demands on the limited resources and priorities of potential donors. It might be advisable, therefore, to consider other supplementary or supportive measures.

One modality could be to encourage regional or subregional organizations to organize meetings on arms transparency in the margins of relevant events, either independently or in cooperation with the United Nations. Another option might be to include arms transparency in the agenda of their regular meetings. The 2006 Expert Group did refer to such supplementary approaches in its recommendations. Perhaps, the reference to such measures could be further reinforced to more fully explore their potential.

VIII. Conclusions

THE REGISTER WAS NOT ESTABLISHED AS AN INSTRUMENT WITH A PREDETERMINED SCOPE but as a potentially dynamic mechanism for promoting confidence-building among States through enhanced levels of transparency. It has moved in that direction through some modifications made to its operation and scope in recent years.

To recapitulate, by lowering the reporting threshold for artillery-systems, the Register demonstrated its adaptability to regional security concerns, since mortars are more widely used in civil conflicts that have been the norm in many regions, rather than traditional inter-State conflicts.

Likewise, by incorporating man-portable air defense systems, known as MANPADS, on an exceptional basis, the Register made its contribution to broad-based international efforts to prevent unauthorized entities, such as terrorists, from acquiring these potentially deadly weapons.

Since the Register operates in a changing security environment, marked by new developments in military technology and methods of warfare, it has to cope not only with existing challenges, which include some long-standing issues, but also with emerging challenges, some of which are likely to loom large in the next 5 to 10 years.

For example, ten years ago combat unmanned aerial vehicles, (UAVs), were just entering the scene and their role in combat operations was very limited. They have become a significant asset in modern warfare. Also, the lethality (range and precision) of conventional munitions — regardless of the platform from which they are fired — have also increased greatly, transforming the battle-field spatially. Meanwhile, new armaments that are in the offing based on directed energy, such as laser weapons and electromagnetic guns, will further change the nature of the battlefield, eroding the central role currently enjoyed by conventional munitions.

The mechanism of periodic review provides a potential safeguard to ensure the Register's continued progress as a transparency instrument. The previous reviews have contributed towards an atmosphere of productive and focused discussion, thereby laying the basis for a constructive examination of the pending issues.

In addition to drawing upon the experience of the review process that has been in operation since 1994, the criteria spelled out in the 1992 report of technical experts also provides important guidelines concerning the Register's further development.

The prospects of consensus building will ultimately determine the results that can be achieved at any particular stage. Since the Register is reviewed periodically, its future is not tied to the outcome of any one review while the periodicity of the review process provides space for consensus-building efforts on a continuing basis. Indeed, the progress achieved on some issues in 2003 and 2006 were related in large part to the work of the previous review.

Those achievements raise the expectation that, through sustained consensus-building efforts, the Register will be able to maintain the momentum for its continued progress.